T0163717

SUCCESSION OR FAILURE

The Small Business Owner's Essential Handbook
for Value Creation, Exit Strategy Planning
and Capital Extraction

KRISTOFOR R. BEHN, CFP®

NEW YORK

SUCCESSION OR FAILURE
The Small Business Owner's Essential Handbook
for Value Creation, Exit Strategy Planning and Capital Extraction

Published in New York, New York, by Morgan James Publishing. Morgan James and The Entrepreneurial Publisher are trademarks of Morgan James, LLC.
www.MorganJamesPublishing.com

The Morgan James Speakers Group can bring authors to your live event. For more information or to book an event visit The Morgan James Speakers Group at www.TheMorganJamesSpeakersGroup.com.

ISBN 978-1-63047-354-9 paperback
ISBN 978-1-63047-355-6 eBook
ISBN 978-1-63047-356-3 hardcover
Library of Congress Control Number: 2014945033

A **free** eBook edition is available
with the purchase of this print book.

CLEARLY PRINT YOUR NAME ABOVE IN UPPER CASE

Instructions to claim your free eBook edition:
1. Download the BitLit app for Android or iOS
2. Write your name in **UPPER CASE** on the line
3. Use the BitLit app to submit a photo
4. Download your eBook to any device

Cover Design by:
Rachel Lopez
www.r2cdesign.com

Interior Design by:
Bonnie Bushman
bonnie@caboodlegraphics.com

Illustrations by:
Todd Mitchell
Mitchellcreativegroup.com

In an effort to support local communities, raise awareness and funds, Morgan James Publishing donates a percentage of all book sales for the life of each book to Habitat for Humanity Peninsula and Greater Williamsburg.

Get involved today, visit
www.MorganJamesBuilds.com.

Habitat
for Humanity
Peninsula and
Greater Williamsburg
Building Partner

SUCCESSION OR FAILURE

*To my wife, who selflessly fuels my ever-expanding
endeavors with her loving, unwavering support,
and to my three children, whom I hope to inspire
to be more in life than they think possible.*

TABLE OF CONTENTS

INTRODUCTION

As an instrument-rated private pilot, I have found many common threads that serve to tie flying an aircraft and operating most any small to midsized business together. The main thread that inextricably links the two is the critical element of continuous improvement. A pilot and a business owner suffer from skills that can rapidly atrophy with each day that passes. In flying, skills are measured in degrees on a compass or in feet of altitude. In business, skills are much more difficult to measure and therefore often weaken to a point of failure without advance notice. Throughout this book I will use my flying experience to convey and simplify complex business concepts so that you can better visualize what lurks in the shadows of your business entity.

We've all looked up to see a small aircraft flying overhead and been intrigued by the sheer physics of how that aircraft holds itself up there. The art of flying is very similar to running a small to midsized business as both flying and running a business are nothing more than a series of tradeoffs. Some fear flying in a small aircraft because they are concerned about that aircraft's sudden departure from flight due to issues beyond their control and the resultant free fall. It is important to note that pilot error is to blame in nearly every incident involving an aircraft. So it stands to reason that, if we boil this fear down to its lowest common denominator, our concern is really based in our inability to control the outcome.

Flying an aircraft begins with a thorough understanding of how the aircraft overcomes the laws of gravity to ascend thousands of feet up. Allow me some latitude to explain the art of flying as it will help you to literally gain a bird's-eye view of your business entity and your influence and ultimately your control over its direction. Learning to fly begins with an introductory flight where you climb into an aircraft that looks and feels like a tin can with an instructor you met moments before. Your initial impression is that you are placing your life in the hands of the instructor in the right seat while you occupy the "pilot's" seat on the left side of the aircraft. Following a brief conversation with the instructor, designed to make you more comfortable with what you are about to do, you turn the key to the right and the propeller comes to life. You don a headset to drown out the noise of the aircraft engine and to aid in communication with the instructor to your right. You are then given simple instructions that your feet control the steering of the aircraft while on the ground and are told to release the parking brake. You are now taxiing the aircraft through a maze of taxiways toward the runway.

After a few minutes of taxiing the aircraft, you get the hang of it and realize that there are two distinct portions of the rudder pedals at your feet. The rudder pedals are comprised of "toe brakes," which allow you to slow and ultimately stop the aircraft and a steering mechanism that allows you to control direction. Inevitably, new pilots (and many experienced ones) use the entire pedal to control both direction and taxi speed resulting in the aircraft lunging right, left, and forward in lurching discomfort. It's similar to driving a stick shift for the first time. From above, similar to an alligator's tail, the back of the taxiing aircraft appears to move much more than the aircraft itself, until the instructor intervenes and advises you that you need only apply easy pressure to the rudder pedals, which smoothes the ride. As you near the end of the taxiway, you are gaining some comfort in the handling of the steering and braking of the aircraft. The nonstop chatter of the instructor has helped to calm your nerves, though you have ignored most of what's been said as you have been focused on avoiding an encounter with the grass that occupies either side of the paved taxiway. You are told to relax as all of this is normal in the process of learning to fly.

Next, the instructor tells you that you are going to test the aircraft systems to ensure the aircraft is safe to fly. *Well, that's comforting,* is your silent thought as the emergency brake is engaged and the engine revs up. Checks are performed according to a time-tested checklist, and once satisfied, the instructor tells you the aircraft is ready to fly. Instructions are conveyed, though again, you have lost focus in the flop sweat that has developed. Before you know it, you are taxiing into position on the runway while the instructor keys the radio to convey your intentions to others in the vicinity of the airport. Once lined up on the centerline of the runway, you are told to release the brakes and apply the power of all 140 horses trapped under the cowling. The aircraft is quick to respond and rolls down the runway gaining speed. You are then told to apply finger-back pressure to the yoke and, once the aircraft reaches about 60 knots, you are airborne in an amazing feat of physics. You are flying!

Now what? Once in the air, the instructor leans over and rotates a small "trim wheel" between your seats and instructs you to take your hands off the controls. You're apprehensive of course, but you comply, and much to your dismay, the aircraft continues to climb and maintains its course. Flight lesson one is largely complete as you realize that aircraft fly themselves and pilots are simply there to guide them. So long as an aircraft has fuel and oil, it will fly until either is depleted or you hit something unforgiving. This is true of our business entities as well. An aircraft uses high-octane aviation-grade fuel to continue running; we use revenue to fuel our business entities. The oil that is used to lubricate engine parts in an aircraft engine is ingenuity in our business entities. The key in both flying and running a small to midsized business is to ensure that we have both sufficient fuel/revenue and oil/ingenuity to stay on course.

So what about navigation? How do pilots and business owners know where they're going? That is really the question and the reason pilots, whether automated or human, are in the cockpit. Pilots, like business owners, are there to guide the aircraft/business entity along a predetermined course and to monitor systems to ensure everything is running in the green. In business as in aviation, running in the red is dangerous and requires a steady hand.

Occasionally, emergencies require diversion in both flight and in business. That's where we must lean on whatever training we have pursued and thus my previous reference to our reluctance to get in the small aircraft to begin with. It's not our fear of flying but our fear of falling that is instinctive. As the saying goes, it's not the fall that kills you, it's the landing. So let's complete our flight lesson with the landing as bringing the aircraft back to earth provides several good business insights as well.

Landing an aircraft is simply departing in reverse order. For the aircraft to come back to earth, you simply line it up with the runway, decrease power, lower the nose and manage velocity all the way to touchdown. The tricky part is managing velocity, as the pitch of the aircraft is clearly now pointed back toward earth. Apply too much forward pressure on the yoke and you speed up; apply too much back pressure and you get dangerously slow, requiring the addition of power to stay in the air. You see, despite what you see in the movies, the yoke is in the aircraft for velocity and directional control, the throttle, which controls engine power, is there to alter altitude. There is a continuous adjustment of pitch and power all the way to touchdown. This is where pilot experience and attention to detail rule the day as weather conditions make each landing unique. A minor distraction can result in a catastrophe given your close proximity to the ground and, in a busy airport environment, distractions are the rule rather than the exception. This is true in business as well as we are continuously interrupted throughout our day.

Managing your lifecycle in business is the same as flying an aircraft. You initially add some fuel before starting up. You fuel the business with revenue and capital induction as you ascend, fly along your intended course, and ultimately bring it in for a safe landing as you exit with a handful of cash. Sounds simple though the vast majority of businesses fail somewhere along their flight path and face an emergency, off-airport landing, or worse. The question is why does this happen to so many small to midsized business owners? The reason is simply pilot error, just like in flying. Through a series of distractions, adverse conditions, or fuel starvation, we find ourselves with red indicators. The real problem is a pure lack of experience and formal training. We don't know what to do when we see the red indicator, and often we wonder how long that red indicator has been blinking at us prior to our recognizing it. Pilots have emergency checklists which, when followed, resolve the most common issues or provide guidance in the event of unresolved issues. Pilots train and train and train for these emergencies and commit the initial responses to rote memory. Business owners have no such checklist and are left to determine the best course of action without the benefit of experience or formal training. Had you seen the flashing red indicator immediately, you'd have had more time to take action. Unlike an aircraft in which those flashing red indicators are very hard to dismiss by careful design, business entities lack evident warning signals requiring you to key in on subtle changes. The result is that business owners fail to counteract an off-course reading and thus drive the business into what is often an unrecoverable situation.

So the question becomes "How do we pay close enough attention to the subtle signals our business entity is trying to convey while avoiding the many distractions in everyday life so that we can navigate our way through the business lifecycle to our eventual retirement?" Let's take a page out of the pilot's playbook and create a working business owner's checklist that will allow us to better manage our business's trajectory.

Chapter 1

STATUP

L et's begin our journey through the business lifecycle at the startup phase. Before we can turn the key in our business to get the propeller spinning, there are a few items we must first verify. Before I'll set foot in a small aircraft, regardless of how shiny and expensive the aircraft is and no matter how experienced the pilot flying alongside me may be, I first verify that the aircraft has sufficient fuel and oil.

To verify these two critical elements required for every flight, a pilot must first know their ultimate destination and the specifications for the aircraft. So too must you as a business owner. Where are you ultimately going? What's your destination? Are the specifications of your business entity capable of taking you there or must you make some modifications prior to embarking on or continuing on your journey?

In my consulting with business owners over the years, I have found that very few have a destination in mind when they set out on their journey. This thought process is foreign to me. I believe every business endeavor must begin not only with a prescribed course but must start with an exit strategy in mind. If you don't know where you are going, how will you know when you arrive? If you fail to consider an exit strategy, what will you do when you must pull the aircraft canopy and eject? Seems like a simple concept, yet, to many, it's obtuse to think about their business progression in this way. While I agree, it's unconventional to consider the end at the beginning, I submit to you that visualizing the end result enables you to envision the process associated with reaching that result. As a pilot, you must first know how long it will take you to reach your destination before you depart. You also must consider a number of "what if" scenarios, not the least of which is "How much extra fuel will I burn if there's a line of aircraft waiting to depart and will the remaining fuel be enough to get me to my destination?" While this is an obvious question for a pilot departing for a flight, isn't this the same question we business owners must ask ourselves as we embark on our journey?

What's your endgame? What are you trying to accomplish?

For some, like good friends of mine that own a very successful seasonal restaurant on the shores of Lake Winnipesaukee in New Hampshire, building a legacy business for their children and grandchildren is the goal, while for others, the goal is simply making enough money to fund their lifestyle. Either way, you must carefully plan your exit strategy early and reconsider it often. Regardless of industry, all successful business owners ultimately face the same set of problems:

- How do I identify and retain key employees that will help me to achieve the level of financial success and day-to-day freedom I desire?
- How will my business continue to operate without me at the controls?
- How will I extract the equity value I have built within my business so that I may retire in the level of comfort I have earned?

As a successful business owner, these issues either already haunt your daily life or soon will. This book is designed to address each of these mission critical questions and provide workable solutions that you can begin to implement in your quest for your ultimate retirement, whether today or long into the future. This book should be read in its entirety before you start down any suggested path as critical information is presented in the latter part of the book and in the case study that may provide solutions to common problems encountered by premature implementers.

Chapter 2

UNDERSTANDING
THE SIGNS

One overlaying concept that is critical in each and every aspect of our lives is one I refer to as "The Excellence Concept"—if you're going to put forth the time and effort to do something, anything, commit to being excellent at it. Stopping short of that point makes whatever you have chosen to put that time and effort into worth less than it ultimately could be. Nowhere is that concept more applicable than in the business environment. Businesses, especially small to midsized businesses where our inputs are amplified due to the size of these entities, either flounder or flourish on the basis of The Excellence Concept alone. Whether you're on the top or bottom rung of your industry, the application of The Excellence Concept determines your continued ascent or your descent. Often this ascent or descent occurs more than one rung at a time, so it is crucial that you not only see the signs but that take the time necessary to understand and absorb the signs.

The airport environment is full of so many confusing and often seemingly conflicting signs, but once understood, there is an undeniable rhythm found at an airport. The same is true for the business environment. Control towers guide taxiing, departing, and arriving aircraft around busy airports, maintaining order, but no such guidance exists for you as a small to midsized business owner. Generally speaking, you are the entire board of directors and represent the entire advisory committee within your business entity. Understanding and interpreting what your business is telling you is a critical part of running your business and knowing that you're the only person that can do this can be overwhelming at times. Burying your head in the sand won't get the job done, so let's get to it.

In order to understand and ultimately interpret these signs, we must first begin by gaining a better understanding of what we are doing day to day within our business entity. It is my belief that all business entities, no matter how complex, large or small, can be distilled to basic business elements. By utilizing simple household examples to convey key concepts, I will attempt to provide insights into the lowest common denominators that will enhance the probability of success in your business.

Every business creates, sells, and collects

Inevitably, there will be some argument about this statement by those unwilling to think outside the box so allow me to explain myself. Few will argue that businesses must sell and collect in order to sustain themselves, but many will contest that there are service-based businesses that create nothing, especially here in the service-focused United States. It is important to remember that prior to the delivery of any product or service, one must first generate or identify an existing opportunity or a need for that product or service and then invent a product or create a service to fill that void.

It is easier for most of us to understand the product application of this concept as there are countless examples of products meeting our needs on a daily basis. Simply grab a can opener from the kitchen utensil drawer and you'll see what I mean. Canning in the early 1900s was performed with jars and lids that when cooled were suctioned sealed. Today, when you reach for a can of tuna fish, you proceed directly to the kitchen utensil drawer and grab a can opener. Cans require can openers. Makes me wonder which came first, the can or the can opener.

Google is such a wonderful way to find these tidbits: According to Wikipedia, the can came first. Preservation of food in tin cans was patented by Peter Durand in 1810, but food had been preserved in tin cans by the Dutch Navy as early as 1772. The patent was acquired in 1812 by Bryan Donkin, who had later set up the world's first canning factory in London in 1813. By 1820, canned food was a recognized article in Britain and France and by 1822 in the United States. The first cans were robust containers that weighed more than the food they held and required ingenuity to open, using whatever tools available. The instruction on those cans read, "Cut round the top near the outer edge with a chisel and hammer."

Necessity being the best motivator, the first can openers were patented 1855 in England and in 1858 in the United States. Those openers were basically variations of a knife, and the 1855 design continues to be produced. The first can opener consisting of the now familiar sharp rotating cutting wheel, which travels around the can's ring slicing open the lid, was invented in 1870, but people found it difficult to operate. A breakthrough came in 1925 when a second serrated wheel was added to hold the cutting wheel on the ring of the can. This easy-to-use design has become one of the most popular can opener models.

The creation of a service opportunity, while somewhat more difficult to identify and often requiring another step or two, when distilled, is really no different from the can opener. Take the day care center for example. A booming franchise opportunity spawned from the desire of the 1950s US housewife realizing her value to the workforce. Today, many two-career households struggle financially to pay the daycare center to keep a watchful eye on their children. More than eleven million children under age five spend a portion of their day, every week, in the care of someone other than their mother. A need was identified and a service was created to fill that need. So, can we agree that every business creates, sells, and collects?

Better or cheaper

Since every business, large or small, creates, sells and collects, how does one business compete with another in offering the same product or service? Distilled to its basic elements, the business that effectively competes does so on the basis of better or cheaper.

To be the best at something is the pursuit of most success-driven individuals. Most small and midsized business owners are motivated self-starters that, when given the choice and opportunity, will work to improve their product or service. This is the front line of business warfare. To compete on product or service quality is head-to-head competition at its best, but competition on this level comes at a price.

Take the delivery of television programming for example. Television has evolved from a simple black-and-white method of disseminating news on a few channels to a fully integrated high-definition surround-sound-infused entertainment experience. Today, we launch space shuttles to repair the satellites from which those high definition images are broadcast. While there is no question about the quantum leap that has been achieved where the entertainment value of this programming is concerned, it has come at a high cost. Make no mistake, the desire and the will to deliver the best entertainment at ever-increasing profit margins has driven all of this, but we have reached the tipping point that undeniably occurs in every business where marginal improvements are almost unrecognizable to the end user. When a product or service has little room for perceivable improvement within the scope of better or cheaper, the business owner is left with no other choice but to enter the price war.

When all else is perceived equal, price is the only basis on which products or services are sold. We see this every day as companies vie for each and every dollar of our disposable income. This is a slippery slope given the costs a business endures to initially compete on quality. In the end, it is the business that retreats from the quality battlefield first and thus wages the price war that gains an edge requiring competing companies to either follow suit or die on the vine. It may take a generation or two for this to evolve but in the end, you are left with fewer consumer options, which starts the cycle of creating new consumer options all over again. The better or cheaper business cycle is simply a multigenerational circular reference.

The hardware store is a perfect example of this concept. Hardware stores have been around since the days of fieldstone walls and wagon wheels. The products and services they offered have changed somewhat, but the concept is exactly the same as it has always been. Within the last several decades, as population density increased around the United States and now worldwide, the provision of hardware products and services became a franchise opportunity. Because often only one of these hardware stores occupied a local market, competition on a price basis did not occur. If you needed a lock washer, you drove over to your local hardware retailer and bought one without true knowledge of or concern for the availability of lower-cost alternatives. While these small hardware store owners are busy selling their excessively marked up nuts and bolts, they are unaware that a larger movement is in the works. The big-box hardware retailers enter the business landscape in the late 1970s and profess both better and cheaper, catching the franchise and single local store owners flatfooted and unprepared to compete for business. As a result, within a few short years, these small hardware retailers begin their quest toward extinction. Trends like this one are not always good for consumers.

In a study conducted by economists John Haltiwanger, Ron Jarmin, and C.J. Krizan for the *Journal of Urban Economics* in 2010, about twelve hundred big-box store openings were analyzed to determine the impact on two sets of independent and small chain businesses in the vicinity—those competing directly with the new big-box and those offering different products and services. For competing retailers, the study found "large, negative effects" on those within a five-mile radius of the new big-box, including a substantial number of store closures, and smaller but still significant impacts on those in a five- to ten-mile radius. As for noncompeting businesses, the study found that big-box stores generate no positive spillover. Nearby businesses offering other products and services neither increased their growth nor expanded in numbers after the big-box opened.[1]

In another study conducted by Garrett Martin and Amar Patel at the Maine Center for Economic Policy in December 2011, on a dollar-for-dollar basis, the local economic impact of independently owned businesses is significantly greater than that of national chains. Analyzing data collected from twenty-eight locally owned retail businesses in Portland, Maine, along with corporate filings for a representative national chain, the researchers found that every one hundred dollars spent at locally owned businesses contributes an additional fifty-eight dollars to the local economy. By comparison, one hundred dollars spent at a chain store in Portland yields just thirty-three dollars in local economic impact. The study concludes that, if residents of the region were to shift 10 percent of their spending from chains to locally owned businesses, it would generate one hundred twenty-seven million dollars in additional local economic activity and eight hundred seventy-four new jobs.[2]

As evidence of the multigenerational circular reference indelibly associated with the better or cheaper business cycle, a few small local hardware retailers have survived, and in 2012 some of the same big-box hardware retailers that once threatened the smaller retailers began to close stores. Those that have survived the onslaught of big-box stores have begun their journey to providing better service as they cannot possibly compete on price. "Adapt or fail" is the mantra chanted in this and many other industries upon which big-box solutions of both the traditional brick-and-mortar variety and more recently the virtual variety, have descended. For consumers, the extinction of the small business in lieu of the large big-box solution seems inevitable and is met with verbal resistance but we consumers vote with our dollars and support the businesses perceived to best meets our needs. This is simply part of the normal cycle, which repeats itself over and over. Just wait, an innovator in the hardware industry will eventually identify a need and create an opportunity to better meet that need. And so it goes.

How can you apply these distilled concepts to your business?

Before continuing on, take a minute to contemplate and answer this one question about your business: Do you compete on quality or price?

———————

If you answered that you compete on both quality and on price, you answered correctly.

Create, sell, and collect better

Improving the efficiency of your processes is essential to your survival in business. This of course requires you to possess a set of formal written processes and procedures that provide step-by-step recipes associated with everything that happens within your business. How can you go about improving the efficiencies of your processes if you have no baseline from which to gauge improvement? Assuming you fall into the large percentage of business owners, both large and small, that do not possess a set of meaningful step-by-step procedures to run your business, you must set out to write them. This will require an investment of time but will pay tremendous dividends as efficiency is achieved.

If you are the sole employee of your business, you are your only resource. You must track and document the steps and time involved in all of the business-oriented tasks you do each and every day. If, however, you have built a business or are a division head of a business that employs others, you will ask each and every employee to document their steps and time as well. The more detail included in these written procedures, the better the opportunity for you to identify opportunities to refine them and gain efficiency within your business. Once this initial data-gathering process is complete, you will have compiled an essential tool that none of your competitors will have taken the time to create. The result of this exercise is a substantial business advantage that would not be possible without this new tool. Be careful with this document, as your competitors would love to benefit from all your hard work.

Before I continue with my next example, allow me to first thank my father. My father spent four years setting his alarm and getting up in the middle of the night to wake me to go to work. Without him doing so, I doubt very much that I would have achieved anywhere near the level of success I currently enjoy. Dad, although I'm twenty years too late in conveying my sincere appreciation, I am eternally grateful for just how instrumental you have been in my success. It is said that before you can truly understand the sacrifices a parent makes for their children, you must become a parent and experience those sacrifices firsthand. That's certainly a true statement for me, and I hope that I can find the courage to make the sacrifices necessary to impact my own three children in the way I now understand my father's sacrifices have impacted my trajectory in life.

The package-delivery business represents a terrific example of just how well the concept of studying and focusing on the minute details allows a worldwide business entity to dramatically improve overall efficiency. I spent four years working the early morning shift in just such an environment while pursuing my bachelor's degree at Boston University. In doing so, I became intimately familiar with both sleep deprivation and a saying I frequently use today running my investment management and financial advisory business: "The trouble with opportunity is that it often comes disguised as good old-fashioned hard work." An investment of time and resources is always necessary to identify and later pursue resultant opportunities. It took many years of real-life successes and failures for me to gain insight into the benefits of what I observed firsthand during those early morning shifts loading and later managing those that loaded the package-delivery trucks. But, in the end, those experiences have led me to a very clear understanding of the benefits of knowing precisely how my business runs.

On the surface, the package-delivery business appears to be about shipping packages and that's clearly the way in which their top-line revenue is generated, but the profit is completely dependent on their ability to manage the time it takes to provide this service. While working in this environment, I observed industrial engineers performing time studies on each and every aspect of the process. From the time it took to pull a package from the large tractor trailers that brought them to the warehouse, place that package on the rollers, allow that package to roll down to the conveyor belt, sort that package at multiple locations within the facility, pull that package from the destination belt, mark it according to the proper street and number codes, walk in the delivery truck, place the package on the proper shelf in the truck, walk back out of the truck, strike the stop counter on the way by—well, you get the picture. Each and every piece of all processes is tracked, monitored, and improved over and over again. It is through this tedious effort that profits are wrung out of the package-delivery process penny by penny. No one part of the process is more important than the last but rather each is dependent on the last. When a bottleneck is encountered, it costs the business money. Distilled to its basic elements, it's as simple as that.

So how does all of this help you to be more in tune with the signals your business is conveying? You too can wring the profits out of your business if you know where those opportunities exist. Take the time to actually read the processes you document and, like the package delivery example, break them down into business segments that make sense to your business, then break them down again and again to as finite a level as you can. For example, take this: marketing process, sales process, manufacturing process, service process and then break these down further into *parts* of the marketing process, sales process, manufacturing process, service process, etcetera.

Critically dissect each one of these procedures with an eye toward making them more time and cost efficient. Involve the employees impacted by the procedure in the discussion about efficiency. Often the best way to improve a process is to ask those closest to it to candidly and openly convey what can be done to make their job function more efficient and easier for them. You'll be amazed what employees will tell you if you ask for their involvement and actually take the time to listen to what they have to say. Who knows, you may even become an innovator within your own industry segment by unearthing an opportunity nobody has invested the time to identify.

An Efficiency Checklist Template for your reference can be found in the Appendix.

Chapter 3

SYSTEMS GO, READY FOR DEPARTURE

F ollowing a thorough check of the systems, a pilot tunes into the control tower frequency on the radio, listens for an opportunity to communicate without stepping on another pilot communication and conveys a readiness to depart to the tower controller. Once cleared, the pilot looks up at the final approach course to verify that the area is clear of arriving aircraft and then taxis out to the centerline for departure.

Now that you have a better understanding about how your business functions and where efficiencies can be achieved, it's time to make some difficult decisions. After you have collected sufficient data to objectively analyze your business processes, sit down with a knowledgeable advisor that knows little about your business or your industry. You are looking for an objective, independent review of the data you have gathered. Because one must protect themselves these days, ask them to sign a nondisclosure agreement (NDA). Most any business attorney can provide a boilerplate document that will at least serve as a deterrent to that individual using the information you share. I know it sounds silly, but you'd be amazed at the true lack of integrity in the business environment these days.

A sample Nondisclosure Agreement (NDA) can be found in the Appendix.

Most business owners simply do not have good working knowledge of their company's financial books. Your name need not be followed by the initials "CPA" to gain an understanding of where your profit centers and cash drains exist. In fact, formal accounting education can lead to a large business approach that isn't all that helpful when looking under the hood of a small to midsized entity. Dissect your books or engage a quality accounting professional to help you do so. Highlight the areas where your true profits are achieved. Note that these may well surprise you as many small to midsized business owners focus on the areas that generate the most top line revenue rather than those that result in the highest bottom line profit. Take a critical look at just how successful your business really is or may become. False grandeur is a waste of time for all involved, so let's be sure you have a business successful enough to stand the test of time.

- Action Step: Financial Analysis—This will take an investment of time but is perhaps the best way to wrap your hands around the controls of your business.
  - ◊ First, create a meaningful balance sheet for the last three years. A balance sheet is a snapshot of your company's financial condition. It is comprised of three basic parts: assets, liabilities, and ownership equity.
  - ◊ How much does your balance sheet differ from year to year? Is it improving? What conclusions do you reach about the health of your company following this initial stage of trend analysis?
  - ◊ Next, create an income statement (P&L) for the last three years, with percentages of total revenue/expense. An income statement (P&L) displays your company's revenue and expenses by category. Attempt to categorize your cash flow into two distinct categories: recurring revenue/expenses and nonrecurring revenue/

expenses. By creating a properly categorized income statement (P&L) with percentages of revenue/expense, you can more easily see where your revenue is generated and spent, thereby leading to your resultant profit margin.

◊ What trends can you identify over the three-year period? The easiest trend to identify should be the direction and consistency of your profit margin. Are you selling more or less of a particular product/service this year over the last year or two? What expenses have increased/decreased the most? How do those trends impact your profit margin?

◊ Translate this information into meaningful ratios.

◊ What is your profit margin?

◊ How much do profit margins vary from year to year?

◊ How much must you spend to create each dollar of revenue?

◊ Evaluate your business.
  o Operational efficiencies
    ■ Quantify profit centers
  o What are your most profitable products or services?
  o Who are your best customers?
  o Create a list of your employees and their duties.

- Be specific as there may be areas where you can identify overlap of employment duties and therefore operational efficiencies can be enhanced.

o How effective are your marketing efforts?
  - A friend of mine commonly says, "Either your business is growing or slowly failing, you're never standing still."

o What can I do now to maximize the potential of the business?
  - Identify or bring in key employees that can help you to achieve the level of success and freedom you desire.
  - Implement change that will enhance the value of your business.

A Financial Reports Checklist can be found in the Appendix.

Following confirmation of the conclusions you reached during your analysis, it's time to implement the changes that will improve each phase of your business. It's time to make the difficult decisions only you, the business owner, can make. Here are a few examples of some questions you must ask yourself as you continue to dissect each of your business functions:

- Is each product or service profitable individually or must they be offered in a combination to produce profit?
- Is the employee currently running a particular business process the right person for the job? Would you hire this individual for this job function if they applied today?
- Given the domestic and international outsourcing opportunities that exist today, you have to ask yourself this: Can tasks currently handled in-house be more efficiently handled by outsourcing them? This question will require a great deal of research to answer, and the impact of the decision will have varied impact based upon your industry.
- What procedures/processes are missing from your business?
- Could you broaden or streamline your market to better serve your end customer? If so, could you acquire or divest business segments to improve your business?

Chapter 4

NAVIGATION

In order to maintain the delicate balance and rhythm within the airport environment, navigational skills are immediately required following departure from a busy airport as air traffic controllers manage the flow of inbound and outbound aircraft. Navigating your way through difficult business decisions day to day requires both patience and acute focus on your ultimate end goal/exit strategy. Pilots use time-tested old-fashioned "steam gauges" in conjunction with state-of-the-art GPS-linked technology to identify "way points" as a reference to stay on course toward their ultimate destination.

Remember that you must always manage your business entity with the endgame/exit strategy in mind. Doing so will assist you in plotting and identifying your business "way points" along your path. Without both a destination and measurable reference points to gauge your progress, you cannot possibly know how close or how far you are from your endgame/exit strategy.

Assuming your endgame/exit strategy is to eventually monetize and divest your entity either to a child or grandchild or to an internal or external successor, preparing your entity for this eventuality is a critical step. Your investment of time and energy in understanding your business processes/finances and then making those business processes more efficient, will pay off in spades as you prepare to divest your entity. Your efforts translate directly into tangible entity-value enhancement. You see, what you are divesting is not your business but rather the cash flow and ultimately the profits from your business.

As a business owner, your first objective must be to maximize cash flow and ultimately enhance profits throughout your business lifecycle. This becomes particularly important as you approach the exit point since the value of your business entity and thus the total value you can extract from your entity is based entirely on profits not on cash flow. Business owners tend to focus on increasing their cash flow and incorrectly believe that they are making more money. You only make more money or profits if you focus on increasing cash flow in areas that generate profits. This is where you can apply the research you did at the end of the last chapter.

By critically reviewing the financial reports you pulled together, you undoubtedly uncovered some products and services that produce greater profits than others. The uncomfortable part of this review process is that these more profitable products and services are often not those that are your best sellers. If they were, you'd be more profitable. Simple concept, right? We're all creatures of habit. We market and sell what we sell best, not what makes us the most profit dollars. This is not intentional but is all too common in life and in business as we seek the path of least resistance. Since the goal is to create the greatest number of profit dollars, it stands to reason that your focus must become marketing and selling more of your most profitable products and services. Doing so will maximize cash flow, enhance profits, and enable you to increase the value of your business entity.

Your next objective will be to continually enhance profitability as a whole. Process improvements likely became clear in last chapter's critical business analysis.

It is time to probe those areas in an attempt to make broad improvements in your internal processes. Areas for improvement will be evident only if you have done the arduous work associated with documenting your internal procedures. If you haven't taken this step, it's time to sit down and do so as it is without question the place where profits are most likely hiding from you. Like the package delivery business I referenced earlier, continuous review and improvement of your internal procedures allow you to wring out every last profit dollar.

Profits are the net of revenue in and expenses out, so it stands to reason that by reducing expenses you will directly impact profits. This is often the most difficult step in the business enhancement process, as it requires you to look directly at and to cut expense items on your income statement. By creating an income statement with percentages, you now have a magnifying glass through which to view your largest expense items. I would suggest you start there, as the larger the expense item, the greater the impact on your profitability. Don't stop there though, look at each and every expense line item with the goal to place each in one of two categories: essential and nonessential. Essential items are items without which your business will cease to function. Nonessential items are the remainder by default.

An Essential / Nonessential Expense Worksheet example can be found in the Appendix.

Pilots apply a nonstop visual scan of their instruments to monitor flight. By employing this perpetual scan of your business entity, you will ensure you stay on course toward your ultimate goal of value extraction and will be more apt to identify blinking red lights on the dashboard. Whether through the use of technology, labor cost reductions, or something specific to your business endeavor, there are always new cost-cutting measures that can be implemented.

Chapter 5

DEVIATION — HEADWINDS OFTEN REQUIRE REFUELING

P ilots must manage, assess, and ultimately act on many variables along their route of travel. Adverse weather conditions, poorly forecast winds, or an unexpected airport closure may require deviation from our intended destination. Left unaddressed, these unforeseen issues can be disastrous in flight reducing and/or eliminating a pilot's options. With each airport a pilot overflies, a decision is made to continue the flight. As a pilot pushes on, fuel is burned thereby limiting how much further the aircraft can continue under its own power. As this situation progresses, you either reach your destination or hope to find a field in which to safely put the aircraft to rest.

Our small to midsized business entity must be operated in a very similar manner. As resources are exhausted, they must be continually replenished either by ongoing revenue from operations or from additional injections of capital. Unless you have a rich uncle with unlimited resources at your disposal, you should proceed with extreme caution here. If you're anything like me, there is no safety net to break your fall should you stumble. This is part of the fun associated with running a business. Your ability to meet next year's expenses depends entirely upon how well you manage and invest your current working capital.

It is said that banks will only reliably lend to those who lack the need for funds. Stated differently, don't wait until you fall on a rough patch to secure a line of credit to help you manage the ebbs and flows of normal working capital reserves. If you do, you will certainly be declined any access to additional funds. Banks are only willing to go down with ships the size of aircraft carriers like the auto industry of Detroit, Michigan, or the airline industry. There is no shortage of funds available to industries that employ hundreds of thousands of people that are too big to fail until they ultimately fail, and even then the federal government will step in to pour more money down the toilet until it clogs.

Rest assured, you will not receive any bailout funds, so you must plan to help yourself out of a tough spot when one arises. This plan requires either a war chest of cash on hand or access to a credit line. Because every business is different in terms of required on-hand cash reserves, you will need to assess this for yourself. A good rule of thumb is to maintain between ninety days and one hundred eighty days of business expenses in cash reserves, though I recognize this is a tough threshold for most small businesses.

As a Certified Financial Planner, I would be remiss if I failed to warn you of the dangers of financing business activities with personally secured debt but without substantial business assets against which a business line of credit can be collateralized. You are unlikely to have much choice in the matter. So, while times are good, consult a few relatively large local/regional banks with an appetite for commercial lending to determine if and to what extent they will provide a line of credit for working capital purposes.

It is important to have your financial documents in order, as banks will review them with great scrutiny prior to committing funds. It is also beneficial to have a couple of similar institutions competing for your business. Do your homework here to determine which banks are looking to expand their commercial footprint in your local area. Sometimes, receiving an offer from a competitor is all it takes to tip the scale in your favor with the bank of your preference.

Where the type of credit line is concerned, ideally, you are looking for a business line of credit rather than a home equity line of credit. A home equity line of credit can force the sale of your home should you default. A business line of credit, even while personally guaranteed, requires substantially more effort and time on behalf of the bank to collect and thus may provide you with some additional assurance that you can keep your home should you fall on really hard times. Notwithstanding what I've just said, please consult an attorney so that you fully understand the ramifications of personally guaranteeing business debt. Doing so will ensure you are not blindsided.

Recognize that it is easy to get distracted by the day-to-day occurrences in our business entities, but as the owner, you must remain laser-beam focused if you are to achieve your end goal and your ultimate exit strategy. Tradeoffs are inevitable and how soon you recognize and adjust to them are a large part of what separates the successful from the unsuccessful in most every endeavor.

Chapter 6

PREPARING FOR
THE APPROACH

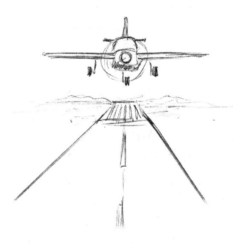

K nowing the destination before departure is critical.
So too is having the necessary information that
will allow you to fly an approach into the chosen

airport. Instrument-rated pilots are required by law to know quite a bit of information about the airport into which they will ultimately fly an approach. While that provides some level of comfort to nonpilots, isn't it simply common sense that one would want to understand as much about their ultimate destination as possible before arrival? Details like whether the airport is open to inbound traffic are important.

I'll share a quick personal story that will help to highlight the importance of this concept. A few years back I flew with my wife and three children from our home base airport in Mansfield, Massachusetts, to Williamsburg, Virginia. We departed at dusk with the plan to land in Williamsburg shortly after dark. As an instrument pilot, I verified that the weather looked good, there were no expected delays along our route, and that the airport was confirmed open. We received our clearance and departed. While briefing the approach into Williamsburg, I noticed that the approach plate, which outlines how a pilot navigates to and ultimately lands at an airport, read, "Approach Not Authorized At Night."

Since it was dark already, as I was handed off to Potomac approach control, I did what most any instrument pilot would under the circumstances and asked, "Is the approach into Williamsburg, Virginia, in fact not authorized at night?" The response was of course, "What does the approach plate say?" followed I'm sure by some off-air chuckling. I confirmed that it indeed said it was not authorized and was asked of my intentions. I advised the controller that I would continue inbound and land visually, which essentially means that I would not fly an instrument approach into Williamsburg. Since I'd never flown into that airport, I was looking forward to the instrument guidance that would provide a breadcrumb approach all the way to touchdown, but instead I was forced to land visually in the dark. I landed without incident, but clearly had I done my homework more thoroughly prior to departure, I would have left earlier so I would have had the benefit of the sunlight.

Fumbling around in the dark is no way to fly an aircraft, and it is certainly no way to run a successful business. Having worked so hard to understand your business processes, refine your financial structure, and ultimately make your business entity more profitable, it's time to prepare to deploy your exit strategy. For our purposes, I'm going to assume that you would like to extract capital from your business entity so that you can either comfortably retire or fund your next project.

Extracting capital from your small to midsized business entity is a delicate process, but not unlike each step that has taken you to this point in your business, understanding what is required and then carefully and deliberately executing is the proper way to proceed. You must answer a number of specific questions at this stage to know if you are really ready to continue forward with your exit strategy or need to go back and further refine your business entity. This is the primary reason you are preparing for your exit strategy before you need to execute it. Doing so allows you the opportunity to go back and fix the issues you uncover. Here is a list of questions followed by a brief discussion of each that will help you to gauge your readiness to continue toward your exit strategy while maximizing value extraction:

Have you documented and refined your business procedures?

I spent a fair amount of time describing why this step is essential to your exit strategy earlier in this book. If you have not yet invested the time and resources necessary to perform this analysis and document the procedures as outlined, I would say you are not yet ready to deploy your exit strategy and would suggest that you read this book again from the beginning. These business procedures will form the basis of how your successor runs each and every aspect of your business. You will benefit the most from the investment of your time in this analysis process. Trust my experience here and get it done.

Is your business entity as nimble and profitable as it can be at this point?

If you have followed along and implemented the prescribed components throughout this book, you have undoubtedly made your business a thriving profit machine. If, however, you are not fully convinced that your business entity is all it can be, by all means, refine it further. Again, you will benefit the most from every profit dollar you wring out of your business entity. The more nimble your business entity is, the better your probability of success in transitioning it will be.

Have you considered all of your options with respect to keeping your business entity rather than transitioning it to a successor?

It should not be a forgone conclusion that your only option is to sell a portion of or all of your business entity. I have consulted with many business owners over the years in an effort to craft a succession plan, and on several occasions, for a variety of reasons, we determined the best course of action is to add a layer of management rather than selling the entity. I don't mean to imply this approach is easier than identifying a successor, because often this option is much more difficult. I'm merely pointing out that you should consider all viable options before settling on one. Remember that your decision is irrevocable and therefore should be made only after having gathered all the necessary information.

Do you have a key employee in mind that would make a viable successor?

It is common for a key employee to rise to the top in a succession planning discussion with a qualified consultant. If you can dismiss your emotional connection to your key employee, you will be a better gauge than anyone else as to the viability of this successor. Dismissing your emotional connection can be very difficult of course, but doing so is critical if you are to assess your employee objectively.

Ask yourself:

Does this employee possess the leadership skills necessary to be an owner?

Do they want to be an owner?

What would their spouse have to say about the additional hours and personal capital they will need to invest to make this work?

Does that key employee have access to funding that would allow you to extract some initial capital, or will you be financing the buyout completely?

In my experience, this is the biggest hurdle associated with succession planning in the small to midsized business environment. It is essential that you understand where the money will come from before you get too far down the path with any potential successor. There are a myriad of ways to finance deals like the one you're considering, but you need to get your hands around which ones are viable in your situation. For example, if you've been so laser-beam focused on running your business entity that you've forgotten to squirrel away some retirement savings, that is a factor that must be considered at this point in the succession planning process. After all, you could theoretically work forever—right? Or perhaps it would be better to get your personal finances in order prior to selling the income-producing asset that makes your life possible. Careful planning will rule the day here. If you're unsure about your personal financial situation, consult an advisor that will help you better understand where you are currently before making any decisions or promises to a potential successor.

Are there regulatory or licensing issues that would delay or prevent your key employee from taking the reins?

Many business entities require regulatory approval or specific licensing before ownership can be obtained. Selecting a successor that due to some past incident or conflict cannot own your entity would prove problematic. It's best to understand any potential hurdle that might delay or prevent your selected successor from taking the reins before you get too far down the path with that individual or entity.

If no viable internal successor exists, are there local competitors that might be interested in acquiring your business entity?

We spend so much time trying to outsmart our competitors that we rarely see them as potential business partners or viable successors. Don't make the mistake of overlooking a wonderful succession opportunity just because you haven't always seen eye to eye on the best way to run a business or market your goods or services. In the end, focus on your exit strategy goal and try to look objectively at your competitors to determine if one of more of them might make a viable successor. I recently consulted with an investment advisory/financial planning firm to develop and execute a succession plan and ultimately recommended, for a number of geographic reasons, that we attempt to break his firm up into pieces and scatter the pieces among competitors. In the end, these bite-sized pieces were much more palatable to the competitors and yielded significantly more exit capital to the exiting owner than would have been possible if the entity remained a single unit. Experience allows for creativity, and unfortunately there just aren't enough experienced succession planning consultants out there in the small to midsized business environment. Tread carefully here.

Have you explored online resources like our matching site, www.SuccessionRegistry.com, to identify potential suitors and to better understand the process?

There aren't many online resources available to small to midsized business owners that are interested in identifying viable successors. I have developed a succession planning website designed to match those wishing to pursue an exit strategy with those who are searching for an opportunity to become an owner. I created this site to fill a void in the succession planning industry segment because such a site didn't exist. On the site you will find a growing list of vetted succession planning consultants. The site may be a valuable resource to you, and I invite you to check it out as you consider your succession planning options.

**Do you have a feel for how much
your business entity is really worth?**

Small to midsized business entity valuation is an art form. It is important to gauge what your entity is worth before you approach a potential successor so as to avoid an embarrassing situation as you move farther down the path. It has been my experience that formal business valuations, while valuable on the surface, fail to take into account the industry specific and entity specific value enhancers and detractors that are inevitably associated with your entity. Again, a qualified succession planning consultant will take the time necessary to understand the nuances associated with your specific industry and entity so that you can obtain the best valuation estimation possible. Remember, a valuation is an opinion of value not an ironclad bulletproof number.

**Would your clients/customers accept your
chosen successor as a replacement for you?**

Remember that it is critical that your clients/customers accept your chosen successor as a viable replacement for you in order for you to fade into the woodwork. Therefore, you must select this individual carefully and must also take steps early and often to lessen your business's dependence on you as the sole point of contact. Doing so will allow for an easier, more seamless transition to your eventual retirement from the day-to-day operations.

How will you transition your client/customer relationships to maximize retention and secure your exit strategy?

Retention of client/customer relationships is the key component to your successful exit strategy. Your ability to extract the necessary capital from your business that ultimately funds your retirement hinges on the retention of client/customer relationships. This is the very reason you must carefully select your successor and proceed deliberately with each step forward in the exit strategy process. Miss a step in a well-thought-out transition strategy and you could lose clients/customers. Your clients/customers must see your chosen successor as a step up for them. Be it better service, more current knowledge, or better use of technology, you must take a stance and sell that stance in every conversation you have, every marketing message you convey, and every action you take. You must believe it to sell it.

What is the contingency plan should something go wrong shortly after you announce your decision to move on to your clients/customers?

Things do go astray from time to time. Contingency plans should be the norm rather than the exception in business as a whole, but when it comes to exiting your business entity, leave nothing to chance. This is where an unlimited number of "what if" questions should be asked. Among others, ask questions like:

- What if my chosen successor loses interest in this endeavor?
- What if my chosen successor becomes ill or dies?
- What if my chosen successor gets in legal trouble?
- What if my chosen successor gets divorced?

Are you prepared to accept the realities of someone else taking the reins of an entity you have poured your heart and soul into?

This is a very difficult pill to swallow for most small to midsized business owners. You have worked many tireless years to build this entity you are now handing over to someone else to run. If you are unwilling to accept this reality, it is best to identify a different alternative before involving someone else in the process. Perhaps in time you will warm up to the prospect of extracting yourself from the day-to-day operations, but you must be ready for it. If not, the transition of your entity to someone else will be wrought with resistance and resultant problems from the beginning.

What are you going to do with the extracted capital to ensure it is preserved and provides the lifestyle to which you have grown accustomed?

Prior to the exit strategy funds flowing to you, it is very important for you to have a plan for how these funds will be handled.

- Do you pay down debt, invest the funds, or some combination of the two?
- What's the most efficient tax strategy for you?
- Can you do a better job negotiating terms of your exit strategy so they are more beneficial to you from a tax perspective?
- Who can you turn to for truly objective advice without the product sales pitch?

Having been in the investment advisory and financial planning business for decades, I would like to share a couple of indisputable facts. There are two types of investment advisors/financial planners:

- Commission-based/fee-based salespeople
- Fee-only investment advisors/financial planners

Allow me to explain the difference between the two. Commission-based/fee-based salespeople have an incentive to sell you products and services that may or may not be aligned with your stated goals and objectives. This is true of any industry but, given the strength of political lobbyists in the insurance/investment advisory/ financial planning environment, nowhere is this more dangerous. Products have their place within financial plans, but I would submit to you that they should never, ever drive the plan. Fee-only investment advisors/ financial planners are free from incentive conflict. Fee-only advisors are paid to provide objective advice and do not place product sales and therefore will not allow products to drive planning considerations.

Given the two options, the choice is very clear in my opinion. It is the reason I have resided on the fee-only side of the industry since I started my investment advisory and financial planning firm, the Fieldstone Financial Management Group. Offering Advice. Not Products™ is the only way to ensure that you are receiving truly objective guidance rather than a product sales pitch. So when deciding what to do with the proceeds that are the result of a lifetime of hard work, I would suggest that you work with a fee-only investment advisory/financial planning firm.

We have done some of that vetting for you on the Succession Registry site. By visiting www.SuccessionRegistry.com, you can peruse and contact a list of qualified fee-only advisors to help you safeguard your hard-earned extracted capital. Please use this list merely as a point of reference and conduct your own interviewing/vetting. Circumstances of advisors change, and I cannot vouch for any firm other than my own in this capacity.

What do you plan to do with all your free time?

Now that you have stepped aside from the day-to-day operations within your business and have hired a qualified fee-only advisor to help ensure you are making the most of your extracted capital, what will you do to keep yourself busy? It is important to stay active as you walk away from the hustle and bustle of your business. All too often people retire and become sedentary and health problems seem to be the result. Remain actively involved in mentally and socially stimulating activities. Look at your transition into retirement as simply an alternative to work rather than an opportunity to sit on the couch. Take the trip you were never able to take because work got in the way. Stay engaged in life, and you'll age more gracefully.

Chapter 7

TOUCHDOWN
AND THE ROLLOUT

t is said that any landing you can walk away from
is a good landing, but let's face it, we all measure
the skills of the pilot by how smoothly the tires
grease along the runway upon the much-anticipated
touchdown. The same is true for a well-thought-out
carefully executed exit strategy. The better prepared

you are, the smoother your transition will be. It's that simple. Structuring your exit strategy is an art form. This is where a qualified succession-planning consultant can really add value to the equation. Again, by visiting www.SuccessionRegistry.com, you can acquaint yourself with a growing list of qualified succession-planning consultants. Again, conduct your own due diligence in hiring a consultant. Nevertheless, I will provide some guidance here that will help you to understand the financial underpinnings of most any exit strategy.

First, it is important to recognize that no successor, no matter what the long-term opportunity looks like, will work for any period of time without compensation. Put yourself in that position: Would you? It is a common misconception that if the opportunity is strong enough, someone will see the opportunity and will be willing to jump in to learn the ropes without compensation. You must be willing and able to carve out a reasonable wage for your successor, or the reality is you simply won't have one.

Second, you must be realistic about what your business is really worth. If you have followed the detailed assessment process I laid out earlier in this book, you have done all you can to refine and enhance your business operations and thus your profits. Ultimately it is the sustainable profits, not cash flow, that any successor is interested in and thus what forms the true valuation of any business no matter how big or how small. In the years prior to executing an exit strategy, you will have done everything you can to augment your business so that it is producing maximum profits. This will make paying a successor a reasonable wage that much more viable as I mentioned a moment ago.

Finally, the stronger your client/customer relationships are, the better they will transition to your successor. The strength of the transition to your chosen successor translates directly into how comfortable you will be in structuring the financial terms of your exit deal. If you have done as I suggested and documented each operational component within your business, you'll be that much more likely to successfully transition your business and will worry less about getting paid as the transition progresses. After all, once you've made the decision to walk away and have been assured that your clients/customers will be well looked after, your greatest concern is the security of the stream of cash payments that follow the sale of your business.

Let's look at some common buyout traits that might become a part of your exit strategy structure.

Skin in the game

Traditionally, a down payment is a part of any business succession transaction. This is really a function of a seller wishing to extract some initial capital to secure the transaction and to ensure the buyer has some skin in the game from the beginning. Be honest with yourself about your rationale for a substantial upfront cash payment. Are you requiring one because you need the lump sum of money? Are you unsure about the success of the transition? Is this requirement more emotional than financial? Unless your successor is a Fortune 500 company, banks are rarely a funding option in these types of transactions. So recognize that not all successors will have sufficient liquid cash to make a hefty down payment, and your insistence on one may substantially limit your successor pool.

I have consulted on and participated in deal structures both with and without upfront cash. My observation is that while cash up front certainly makes you feel better in the beginning, deal structures that do not contain a large upfront cash component are far more lucrative in the end. The reason for this is twofold: You broaden the potential pool of successors by limiting the upfront cash requirement and successors are far more likely to agree to longer and richer earn-out terms if their upfront cash contribution to the deal is limited. As a result, you generally end up with a better, more qualified successor and more money if your selection criteria is focused less on upfront cash and more on the retention of your customers/clients.

Earn-out

An earn-out or shared revenue component of an exit strategy is, in my opinion, where the most emphasis should be placed in structuring the deal. This is where a fair amount of flexibility can be exercised and, unless you've structured an all-cash deal, this is ultimately where the lion's share of your extraction of capital will occur. Essentially, an earn-out or shared revenue component of an exit strategy is a payment spread out over several years and simply allows you and your chosen successor to split ongoing revenue subject to contractual terms. These shared revenue agreements generally range from three to ten or more years, depending on the type and size of your business entity. There is really no one-size-fits-all approach, which allows you to custom-tailor the approach.

Boiled down, earn-out or shared revenue agreements are really a simple stream of cash payments, which when calculated equate to a current sum of money. Assuming all else is equal, this is similar to traditional lottery payouts. If you elect the lump sum payment following the presentation of your winning ticket, you receive, say, one million dollars. If you elect to receive your winnings over several years, you receive about the same current value of money spread out over several years, but the actual money received is more than the one million dollars. The mathematical term for this is "net present value," which is achieved through discounting cash flows.

Let's look at a few simplified exit strategy structure examples assuming a one million dollar business valuation, initial recurring annual revenue of $300,000, and 5 percent annual revenue growth:

Exit strategy structure with upfront cash

In this first example, the successor makes a $300,000 down payment and agrees to a 60 percent/40 percent revenue share arrangement for a period of four years. Due to the down payment, the seller agrees to forgo participation in revenue increases during the buyout period. Here's the cash flow by year, including the down payment made at the beginning of year one:

$ 300,000 received by seller at deal consummation

$ 180,000 received by seller in year one (60% of $300,000)

$ 180,000 received by seller in year two (60% of $300,000)

$ 180,000 received by seller in year three (60% of $300,000)

$ 180,000 received by seller in year four (60% of $300,000)

$1,020,000 received by seller throughout buyout

Exit strategy structure without upfront cash

In this example, the successor makes no down payment and agrees to a 75 percent/ 25 percent revenue share arrangement for the first two years, a 60 percent/ 40 percent revenue share arrangement for years three and four and a 25 percent/ 75 percent revenue share arrangement for years five, six, and seven. The successor agrees to allow the seller to participate in the 5 percent annual revenue increases during the buyout period. Here's the cash flow by year:

$ 225,000 received by seller in year one (75% of $300,000)

$ 236,250 received by seller in year two (75% of $315,000)

$ 198,450 received by seller in year three (60% of $330,750)

$ 208,373 received by seller in year four (60% of $347,287)

$ 91,163 received by seller in year five (25% of $364,651)

$ 95,721 received by seller in year six (25% of $382,884)

$ 100,507 received by seller in year seven (25% of $402,028)

$1,155,464 received by seller throughout buyout

Exit strategy with a 30/30/40 approach

In this example, the successor makes a 30 percent down payment, pays 30 percent through earn-out in three 10 percent annual payments and makes a final 40 percent payment on the basis of practice valuation at the end of a predetermined time period. In this case, we'll assume a five-year agreement with an initial payment at closing and annual payments equal to 10 percent of the year-end practice valuation based on a predetermined formula following the end of each of three calendar years. At the beginning of year five, the buyer will make a final payment equal to 40 percent of the practice valuation based on a predetermined formula, thereby ending the buyout phase.

$ 300,000 received by seller in year one (30% of $1,000,000)

$ 105,000 received by seller in year two (10% of $1,050.000)

$ 110,250 received by seller in year three (10% of $1,102,500)

$ 115,762 received by seller in year four (10% of $1,157,625)

$ <u>486,202</u> received by seller in year five (40% of $1,215,506)

$1,117,214 received by seller throughout buyout

Comparing the three simplified examples, over the buyout period, the exit strategy structure without upfront cash yields $135,464 more than the exit strategy structure with the $300,000 down payment, and the 30/30/40 approach provides middle ground. These value differences represent a risk premium paid by the successor to offset the lack of down payment funds and/or overall deal structure. Again, how you structure your exit strategy buyout depends on many factors, not the least of which is confidence in your chosen successor to get the job done.

Regardless of your approach to financing the deal, you'll need a qualified attorney to document each and every detail associated with your transaction. A good contract lawyer is critical here, but I would suggest that you retain the negotiation responsibilities. Lawyers are often so interested in the legal aspects of these contracts, they sometimes forget that people are involved and inflict unintended strain on the relationship between buyer and seller. Speaking from personal experience, since this is likely the beginning of your relationship with your successor, it is best to maintain a cordial dialogue rather than a term-driven adversarial dialogue.

I have conveyed a substantial amount of information within this handbook in the hopes that my having done so will enable you to better understand the key tenants of operating and ultimately exiting from your small to midsized business. My hope is that you now have an appreciation for the need to run your business with an exit strategy in mind. In the end, there are only two options: Succession or Failure.

ABOUT THE AUTHOR

Kristofor R. Behn is an entrepreneur and self-proclaimed businessman. Applying fundamental merger and acquisition strategies common in large corporations, Kristofor pioneered an acquisition strategy in the financial planning and investment advisory space beginning in 2000, long before other advisors considered it a viable strategy for business growth. Kristofor has spent the better part of the last two decades developing and refining all aspects of his financial planning and investment advisory business and has worked to perfect his practice acquisition strategy.

Despite a lack of suitable funding options for practice acquisitions, as of the date of this edition, Kristofor has managed to successfully complete more than six acquisitions and consulted on countless others. Having resolved the merger and acquisition funding issue, today

Kristofor is forging ahead full throttle in pursuit of practice acquisition and succession planning consulting opportunities.

Kristofor is a husband, parent to three children, instrument-rated private pilot, author, and an Ironman distance triathlete.

APPENDIX
CASE STUDY

This case study is a compilation of several succession plans that I have consulted on and implemented so that I can convey best practices in a concise working example. The names of the firms and the details associated have been altered somewhat to protect the privacy of the individuals/ entities involved in the transactions. This case study should not form the basis for your succession plan but should rather form the basis for a more thorough understanding of the information contained within this handbook.

Our case study involves the succession of a recurring-revenue, practice-based business, though much of what is conveyed in this case study is applicable to most any small to midsized business. Our practice owner was fifty-five years old at the time she began to consider her exit from her practice-based business. She had run a fairly efficient technology rich practice and had leveraged outsourced resources wherever possible to enhance profitability. As such, she had a small number of employees who would remain in place following the sale of the business, making the transition to the successor one of simply transitioning client relationships/trust to the successor.

Our practitioner made a number of confidential calls to industry contacts she trusted and quickly learned of a number of business owners interested in growing their practices. Unlike the stock market, where shares are priced and traded daily, the problem at the time of this succession was that no established confidential marketplace like www.SuccessionRegistry.com existed, and therefore our practitioner was largely on her own in identifying well-matched potential successors.

After a number of months, our practitioner selected a few viable successors with whom to share a confidential profile of her firm. As I'm sure you can understand, this is a delicate stage as you are conveying information about your business entity to a likely competitor. Therefore, before sharing this information, a nondisclosure agreement should be executed to protect that confidential information. In this case, a nondisclosure agreement was in fact executed.

Much like a job interview process, following a number of phone conversations to further qualify interested professionals, face-to-face meetings with the handful of potential successors were scheduled. As with any job interview, preparation on the part of the employer and potential employee is necessary so that you each convey the desired level of professionalism. We've all been involved in job interviews where either the candidate or the employer show a clear lack of preparation, and it's a disaster. It's best to avoid that outcome through proper preparation.

After selecting what looks like the perfect successor, due diligence begins. Due diligence is a fact-finding and confirming mission for both sides. Ronald Reagan often used the phrase "trust but verify." Nowhere is that saying more applicable than in the due diligence phase of succession planning. Following the completion of successful due diligence, negotiations begin to establish a workable valuation and deal structure. This is where you want to retain control over the negotiation and use contract lawyers to document your agreements. Using a lawyer to negotiate deal terms on your behalf is an expensive error in judgment that, in addition to the hourly wage you pay the attorney, may cost you the deal itself. For this case study, we used the 30/30/40 approach outlined earlier in this handbook. Rather than repeating that information here, simply reference the prior section for those details.

While there were unexpected bumps along the way, including some unanticipated cash flow constraints that are simply a part of everyday life, the exit of our practice-based business owner went as planned. By the time our practice owner reached age sixty, she had been fully paid for the practice-based business she had built and because the deal structure allowed for her participation in revenue growth, she continued to refer business opportunities to her successor. In succession planning and in life, you must expect the unexpected and maintain a level of flexibility and reasonableness when curve balls are thrown your way. This process is never perfect and how we elect to adapt to changing circumstances defines our outcome.

Checklists/Sample Documents/Worksheets
Follow the links below for access to specifically referenced checklists, sample documents, and worksheets.

www.SuccessionOrFailure.com/EfficiencyChecklistTemplate
www.SuccessionOrFailure.com/
    SampleNonDisclosureAgreement
www.SuccessionOrFailure.com/FinancialReportsChecklist
www.SuccessionOrFailure.com/Essential-
    NonEssentialExpenseWorksheet

Additional resources are also available by visiting
    www.SuccessionOrFailure.com and
    www.SuccessionRegistry.com

REFERENCES

http://ideas.repec.org/p/nbr/nberwo/15348.html
http://www.mecep.org/view.asp?news=2003

Printed in the USA
CPSIA information can be obtained
at www.ICGtesting.com
JSHW080006150824
68134JS00021B/2315

9 781630 473549